Frankfurt in 3 Days:

The Definitive Tourist Guide Book That Helps You Travel Smart and Save Time

"Finest City Guides"

Book Description

Once you decide on a destination for your next vacation, the last thing you want to do is spend more time planning it than the three days you have allotted for the trip itself.

Frankfurt in 3 Days does so much of the research for you. Don't waste time finding restaurants or hotels that may actually now be closed. That's how old a lot of the information online can be. We give you clear descriptions and price ranges for places that you can count on when you get to Frankfurt.

We do all the advance planning for you, leaving you more time to spend exploring the attractions when you arrive. We offer:

- Hotels in three price ranges
- What type of currency you need
- How to get from the airport to the center of town
- Restaurants of all types of cuisine, divided into price points

- The best dishes each restaurant in the book offers
- The liveliest night spots, if you'd like to enjoy the nightlife
- The best attractions – well-known and not so well-known
- Getting around town like the locals do

We make your short trip to Frankfurt stress-free. You can enjoy the best spots the city has to offer.

The People of Frankfurt

The 2015 population of Frankfurt was 731,095. The full urban area has a population of 2.5 million. According to demographic forecasts, the city will have 825,000 in its administrative area by 2020.

What are the people of Frankfurt like?

German people like the rules they live by. It may seem to you that there are rules for every aspect of life. You will want to abide by their quiet time (typically between 1PM and 3PM on weekdays and most of the time on Sundays), if you're in a residential neighborhood. Stay on the paths in parks, not cutting across the grass.

Germans are quite direct, and they feel as though they are always right. Most of them don't have any problems in telling you the way they feel about anything. Arguing with a German is a waste of your time. Just nod and move on.

Germans have a love affair with their cars and the autobahn. Cars in Germany are status symbols, and if there is no traffic on the autobahn, they can hit some frightening speeds.

Germans are excellent hosts and they know how to party. When you sit with Germans in a restaurant, you can bet they will include you in their conversation, if you express an interest.

Language
The official language in Frankfurt, of course, is German, but you'll notice words and phrases in

town that you can understand from your high school German classes. Actually, most people in Frankfurt speak in the Frankfurterisch dialect. If you learn a bit of German before your leave, it will help you, and the locals appreciate it when you try to speak their language, even a little.

In tourist, business and professional circles, most citizens speak English, too. This is especially true in the center of town.

Holidays

January 1	New Year's Day (Neujahrstag)
January 6	Epiphany (Heilige Drei Könige)
Feb – March	Karnivale
April	Good Friday (Karfreitag)
April	Easter
April	Easter Monday
May	Labor Day (Maifeiertag)
May	Ascension Day
(Christi Himmelfahrt, 40 days after Easter)	
June	Whit Monday (Pfingstmontag)

June	Corpus Christi (Fronleichnam)
August	Peace Festival
August	Assumption Day (Maria Himmelfahrt)
October	Oktoberfest
October	Day of German Unity (Tag der Deutschen Einheit)
October	Reformation Day (Reformationstag)
November 1	All Saints' Day (Allerheiligen)
December 25	Christmas Day (Weihnachtstag)
December 26	Boxing Day/St Stephen's Day (Stephanstag)

Religious Beliefs

Originally, Frankfurt was dominated by the Protestant religions. However, during the 1800s, many Catholics moved into the city. The Jewish community of Frankfurt dates to Medieval times, and always ranks among the highest in Germany. There are two synagogues in Frankfurt.

In 1960s, the city began to see a growing number of Muslims immigrating to Frankfurt. Their

Muslim community is large. The largest mosque in the city, the Ahmadiyya Noor Mosque, was built in 1959 and is the third largest mosque in the country.

The largest of Christian denominations in 2013 were Roman Catholics, at nearly 23% of the Frankfurt population, and Protestantism, which has over 19%. It is estimated that Muslims make up about 12%, as of 2006. The Jewish community accounts for about 1% of Frankfurt's population.

Here is a quick preview of what you will learn in this tourist guide:

- Helpful information about Frankfurt
- Flying into the city
- Transportation tips in town
- Why Frankfurt is such a vibrant tourist spot and what you will find most remarkable about it
- Information on luxury and budget accommodations and what you'll get for your money

- The currency used in Frankfurt
- Tourist attractions you should make time to see
- Other attractions for entertainment and culture
- Events that may be running during your stay
- Tips on the best places to eat & drink for all price points, whether you want simple fare, worldwide dishes or German flavor

Table of Contents

Introduction 1

1. Key Information about Frankfurt 8

2. Transport to and in Frankfurt 12

3. Accommodations 19

4. Sightseeing 26

5. Eat & Drink 30

6. Culture and Entertainment 37

7. Special Events in Frankfurt 41

8. Safety in Frankfurt 45

Conclusion 46

Introduction

Frankfurt am Main (pronounced in German as "Frankfurt am Mein") means "on the river Main"). It is the fifth largest German city, and the largest in its state of Hesse. It is an ethnically and culturally diverse city, and many young people have a migration background. About 25% of the population is made up of foreign nationals, and this includes many expats.

Frankfurt is a global hub of transportation, tourism, education, culture and commerce. Many European and global companies have their corporate headquarters there. They hold major trade fairs, auto shows, music fairs and the largest book fair in the world.

A Brief History of Frankfurt

The city of Frankfurt has survived plagues, fires, wars and occupation. The one constant is their resilience. From its first fair in 1157 to its 1998 becoming the home of the European

Central Bank, it has been a financial center for Germany.

The city was originally called Franconovurt, which means City of Franks, as far back as 794. Evidence suggests that the cathedral hill of the city was continuously settled all the way back to 3000 BC.

In AD83, Rome established a military camp in the town, and the city was named permanent home for Roman Kings onward from 1356. Stable years saw the stock exchange begin its trading late in the 1500s, but the city was occupied by the Swedish by 1614.

In the 1630s, which saw an outbreak of the plague, thousands of people died. More perished in fires that burned the Jewish area of the city in 1711 and again in 1721.

Frankfurt began to establish its modern cultural and economic value between the years 1879 and

1914. Its opera house was opened in 1880 and their Goethe University opened in 1914.

Frankfurt's main railroad station was completed in 1888, and the ease of access allowed the population to grow by more than 300,000 in about 30 years. The mayor, Franz Adicke, promoted the city as an industrial hub for trade. The Deutsche Bundesbank moved its operations to Frankfurt in 1957, and other banks followed.

The city was severely bombed by the Allied forces during WW II, but the cathedral and some Römerberg area buildings were reconstructed. The work has been ongoing to rebuild the Old Town, between City Hall and the cathedral, and is slated to be completed in 2017. It is now a cosmopolitan city, with about 180 different nationalities calling it home.

Neighborhoods

We'll tell you here about the neighborhoods you'll be most likely to stay in and explore.

The City

Frankfurt is a compound city, and you can easily walk its center in a day. The heart is called City, and it has about 12,000 residents. It includes the Zeil, a pedestrian-only shopping street and some other streets with shops. Further to the south, you will find Paulskirche, and the historical heart of the city, the Römer. This was rebuilt following WW II.

The Banking District

This is home to the largest banks of Germany, and it doesn't sound like a tourist destination. However, its skyscrapers dominate the skyline, and some are accessible by tourists. A couple even have bars on their top floors, where interested travelers can sip a drink and enjoy the city views.

Sachsenhausen

This is the southern part of the city, and a rather large area. About 56,000 people live in this district. The old part of the neighborhood is a party and tourist center. Traditional bars here offer all types of beverages and food. On the weekends, the area may become very crowded with drunk teens walking from one bar to the next, so it's a good place to avoid at those times.

On Main River's south shore, a sub-area, Museumsufer, has small and medium museums for many types of special interests. Schweizer Platz is a pleasant sub-neighborhood with restaurants that offer tasty foods from many different nationalities.

The Südbahnhof area should be mentioned, since it holds numerous Apple Wine bars. This is the favorite drink of many people in Frankfurt. There are also smaller sized basement clubs here, where you can party on the weekends without competing with teenagers who have had too much to drink.

Westend

26,000 people call this neighborhood home. Art Nouveau houses spared in WW II can be seen here. There are also numerous bars and restaurants that offer special foods, with equally special prices.

We must also mention an area known as Bahnhofsviertel, which is home to 2,350 residents. It's small, but you will probably arrive first here, since it is the location of the main railway station. Day trips for tourists often begin here, as well.

This area is also the home of the red-light district of Frankfurt. There are seedy hotels and bars, along with adult cinemas. It's not truly dangerous, physically, but the drug scene makes it uncomfortable for tourists.

Just several streets north and south of the red-light district are where the tourist hotels start appearing. They offer easy access to Frankfurt's public transportation system.

What does Frankfurt offer its Visitors?

Frankfurt am Main is an international and dynamic trade fair and financial city, with an imposing skyline. Close to those skyscrapers, you will find cozy Ebbelwei pubs and historical sites.

Frankfurt is called the Cradle of German democracy, and the Kaiserdom Cathedral is found there. There are many historical destinations, galleries, museums and gardens in and near Frankfurt, which will turn your vacation into an interesting experience.

The city of Frankfurt has been a center of tourist and cultural activities for a long time. It boasts a complex for trade fairs, called Messe Frankfurt, which hosts important events like the Frankfurt Book Fair, which is the most important publishing event in the world.

1. Key Information about Frankfurt

Money Matters

Germany is a member country of the European Union and uses the euro as its currency. The euro is sub-divided into 100 Euro cents.

Notes are issued in denominations of €5, €10, €20, €50, €100, €200 and €500. Each note has a unique color.

Coins are issued in 1 cent, 2 cents, 5 cents, 10 cents, 20 cents, 50 cents, €1 and €2 denominations.

Credit Cards

Germans mainly deal in cash transactions. They prefer not to go into debt, if they don't have to. Frankfurt has fewer businesses that accept credit cards than other tourist cities in Europe.

Credit cards, however, are accepted at almost all the hotels here, and in some popular tourist restaurants. If you plan to pay for a bar or restaurant bill using a credit card, it's a good idea to check first and make sure the establishment accepts plastic.

Where credit cards are accepted, they generally only use MasterCard and Visa. You may use Diner's Club, American Express or Discover cards in some larger hotels, but not at many other places. This is not intended to slight Americans, but rather is caused by the high processing fees the businesses have to pay when customers use those other "brands" of cards.

Tipping

Tipping is quite often seen in Frankfurt hotels. The hotel employees do indeed expect to be tipped. If your service was good, you should plan to tip the housekeeper three to five euros per night and the porter one to three euros for each bag he carries. If you receive help from the hotel concierge, the tip is often between 10 and 20 euros.

Restaurant Tipping

Those who dine in Germany are of differing opinions about proper tip amounts. Leaving 10% is acceptable on a 10-euro bill, if the service was good. If you only order beer or a small food item, 5% is fine. If your server was exceptional, you could even leave 15%.

The "tip" is technically included in the bill already, marked as "Bedienung." Because of this, some people tip less than 10%, and there really is no established proper amount. If you experience bad service, you can leave a small tip or no tip.

In the United States, you probably leave the tip on your table as you leave. In Germany, the wait staff will not expect you to do this. Some feel that it's rude. Rather, they will let you know your total bill and stand by your table so that they can make change for you. They usually have change purses, so it's easily done.

After you receive the bill, let them know how much money you want back, having factored in the tip you plan to leave. If your math skills don't translate well to euros, or if the server does not understand English well, you can just pay the bill, accept your change and then hand the server your tip amount.

2. Transport to and in Frankfurt

Getting to Frankfurt by Plane

Frankfurt Airport is also known as Rhein-Main-Flughafen. It covers over 4900 acres of land, with two passenger terminals. It's the busiest passenger airport in Germany, and served more than 61 million passengers in 2015.

Getting to Frankfurt from the Airport

You can access the airport by bus, train, taxi or car, and one of its positive features is its extensive network for ground transport. The airport has two railway stations, one for regional and local trains and one for longer distance trains.

Coaches and Buses

Numerous transport companies offer bus service to the airport from surrounding regional areas in and near Frankfurt.

Railway

Frankfurt Airport provides an S-Bahn regional train station outside Concourse B at Terminal 1. This offers access to S-Bahn local commuter lines S8 & S9. These trains each depart every 15 minutes in daytime hours and travel eastwards to Hanau Central Station via the Frankfurt Central Station and the Offenbach East Station.

Westbound trains go to Wiesbaden Central Station west through Mainz Central Station (S8 line) or the Mainz-Kastel Station (S9 line) via Rüsselsheim. It takes between 10 and 12 minutes to get to Frankfurt's Central Station from the airport.

Regional Express (RE) trains travel to Würzburg, Saarbrücken or Koblenz. These trains offer additional connections from the airport to the central station in Frankfurt, but arrive less frequently than the S8 and S9 trains.

Frankfurt Rental Cars

You will find major car rental companies in the airport's Car Rental Center, in the Airport City Mall of Terminal 1. The companies include Hertz, Avis, Dollar, Budget, Enterprise, National, Europcar, Buchbinder and Peugeot Open Europe.

The airport is connected to the Frankfurt Kreuz intersection of the Autobahn, and a 10 to 15-minute drive will have you to the center of Frankfurt.

Frankfurt Cabs

Through the Taxi Frankfurt Portal, you can book long-term cabs, or you can hail them directly. You may pre-book premium class vans for up to seven people, or business class services. Rates are fixed at booking.

There are other taxi operators in addition to those more well-known in the area. They are known as private hired vehicles, Boro taxis, minicabs or limo service.

All German taxis have to have visible meters. Fares are all regulated by local law. The rates vary slightly from one city to the next, but there is usually a "drop charge" of €2-3 ($2.18 to $3.26 USD), and then a set rate of €1-3 ($1.09 to $3.26 USD) for each kilometer. If you're going a longer distance, in excess of 2-5 kilometers, you will pay more.

Time spent sitting in traffic is charged at a rate generally between €0.10-0.50 per minute. Fares can also be higher at certain times of day and days of the week.

If you want to use a credit card for your taxi fare, ask the driver as you get in if he accepts them. If you opt for using the mytaxi app in Frankfurt, you can link that to your PayPal account, and thus pay without cash.

Tipping rates for Frankfurt taxi drivers are usually rounded up from the fare, just to make it easier. For example, if you have a fare of 37 euros, you can give the driver 40 euros and let him keep the change for his tip.

Public Transport in Frankfurt

When you plan to use the Frankfurt Public Transportation System (Rhein-Main-Verkehrsverbund), be sure to check the local schedules ahead of time.

Trains are easy to use in Frankfurt, and you can buy tickets at many locations in town at low prices. The trains are easy to use, fast and safe. The maps are fairly clear, and train system employees are happy to help you if you get lost.

You can also travel in Frankfurt by bus. Its routes are different than the train routes, but costs are very comparable. Bus tickets can be bought in the same places as train tickets, and you can also buy tickets right on the bus.

The Frankfurt tramway is a network that is a vital part of the local public transportation system. There are 10 tram lines, as of 2012, and they travel many of the same basic routes as train lines.

Passes & Tickets

Local trains, S-Bahn trains, underground lines, trams and buses all use the same RMV (Rhein-Main public transport) ticketing. One ticket will cover one trip, even if you change from tram to bus or bus to train, etc.

If you plan to take journeys to various sites in the city, you can purchase the All-day ticket. The price is €7.20. They can be used any time of day, even during peak hours. All-day tickets can be purchased at any ticket machines. Press the 'Tageskarte' button.

When purchasing tickets from a vending machine, here's a great tip. You can switch the language of the machine to English (among other languages) by pressing the small black flag close to the top of each machine.

Some tickets will offer you multiple uses for longer stays, but at present they only offer for one week or more. For three days, you can just use single all-day tickets.

3. Accommodations

You can find nearly any type of hotel or B&B in Frankfurt that you might desire, whether you want to bask in luxury or just rest your head at the end of each day. We have organized them in three price points for your convenience, with a few sample Airbnb locations under the hotels.

We always list the nearby attractions for the hotels in our 3-Day travel guides, so you can more easily choose a hotel that is close to the attractions you want to see most, if you like. Since many of the attractions are in German, we are listing some of them here, before the hotels, translated to English, to help you plan more easily.

Nearby attractions translated to English

- Roemer – Medieval building in Frankfurt
- Messeturm – Trade Fair Tower

- Messe Frankfurt – Exhibition center for fairs, etc.
- Palmengarten – One of two Frankfurt botanical gardens
- Augustinerkirche – part of the local Frankfurt Catholic seminary
- Lilien Carree – shopping mall in Frankfurt
- ZDF – public service television broadcaster
- Museum Wiesbaden – one of three Hessian State museums

Prices for Luxury Hotels: $500 USD to $905 USD per night

Best Western Amedia Frankfurt Ruesselsheim

- Close to Dienst Winery, Franz Kunstler Winery, Open Factory, Ruesselsheim City Park and Opel Villas

Hotel Expo

- Close to Alstadt area, Frankfurt Cathedral, St. Paul's Church and the Museum of Modern Art

Rocco Forte Villa Kennedy

- Close to Main Tower, Frankfurt Cathedral, Frankfurt Opera House and Staedel Museum

Ramada Hotel Frankfurt City Center

- Close to St. Paul's Church, Staedel Museum, Main Tower and the Frankfurt Opera House

Hotel Bliss Frankfurt

- Close to the Financial District, Staedel Museum, Frankfurt Opera House, "Alte Oper" Opera House, Main Tower and Messeturm

Lindner Hotel & Residence Main Plaza

- Close to Frankfurt Opera House, Roemer, St. Paul's Church, Museum of Modern Art and Frankfurt Cathedral

Prices for Mid-Range Hotels: $200 USD to $400 USD per night

Adina Apartment Hotel Frankfurt

- Close to the Financial District, Frankfurt Opera House, Alte Oper Concert Hall, Main Tower, Senckenberg Museum and Messeturm

Le Méridien Frankfurt

- Close to Staedel Museum, Frankfurt Opera House, St. Paul's Church, Messeturm and Main Tower

Innside Frankfurt Eurotheum

- Close to Frankfurt Opera House, Stock Exchange, Alte Oper Concert Hall and Main Tower

Dormero Hotel Frankfurt Messe

- Close to Frankfurt Opera House, Alte Oper Concert Hall, Main Tower, Senckenberg Museum and Messeturm

NAAM Hotel & Apartments

- Close to Alte Oper Concert Hall, Senckenberg Museum, Messeturm, Skyline Plaza, Messe Frankfurt

Hotel Palmenof

- Close to Main Tower, Alte Oper Concert Hall, Messeturm, Senckenberg Museum and Palmengarten

Prices for Budget Hotels: $100 USD or less per night

Hotel Römerstein

- Close to Mainz Cathedral, Kirschgarten, Mainz Carnival Museums and the Church of St. Stephan

Best Western Hotel Amedia Frankfurt Airport, Raunheim

- Close to Dienst Winery, Ruesselsheim City Park, Franz Kunstler Winery, Opel Factory and the Opel Villas

Ibis Mainz City

- Close to Mainz Cathedral, Kirschgarten, Augustinerkirche and St. Ignaz Church

Herrnbrod & Ständecke Hotel

- Close to the Heart of Dreieich, St. Paul's Church, Museum of Modern Art, Frankfurt Cathedral, Commerzbank Arena and the Staedel Museum

Centro Hotel Bristol

- Close to Gutenberg Museum, Kirschgarten, Augustinerkirche and St. Ignaz Church

Hotel am Schloss Biebrich

- Close to Museum Wiesbaden, ZDF, Lilien Carree and Biebrich Palace

Airbnb's

For $33 USD per night, rent a typical small but private room with a comfortable bed. Most have central heat and air conditioning. The location is always important, and the room we're looking at now is in the outer suburbs, just a two-minute walk to the train station. It's also close to restaurants and shops, in a quiet and beautiful area.

$108 USD per night can get you a private room in a centrally-located penthouse. The listing here is for one that is close to the center of town, with easy access to the airport, nightlife, public transport and parks. Outdoor space is a plus, and a comfortable bed is essential.

You can procure an apartment with a living room and balcony for $235 USD per night. The listing we're checking out offers a clean, modern room, with easy connections to the Messe trade fair and the rest of the city, with a central location. This room comes with new amenities, and a private toilet and shower.

4. Sightseeing

Frankfurt am Main, the old city on the River Main, is a vital economic and commercial center in mainland Europe. The skyline of the city is dominated by clusters of skyscrapers. It has a North American flavor, which has resulted in its nicknames of "Chicago on the Main" and "Mainhattan". It's a global city, and usually in the top ten of cities in which to do business and live.

Goethe House Museum

Johann Wolfgang von Goethe was the greatest writer in Germany, and he was born in Frankfurt. His home is a museum, and it is where he was born in 1749 and lived until 1765. It's an excellent example of how wealthy families and their staff lived.

The house itself has many rooms you can explore, from the Dining Room's sumptuous décor to the room where he did much of his early writing, on the building's top floor. Next door, you will find the Goethe Museum, which has 14 rooms that showcase art from his time, including paintings from the Late Baroque and early Romantic periods.

The Museum District
The Museum District in Frankfurt is quite popular with tourists, found on the River Main's left bank. It includes 12 unique museums, many of them well-known internationally.

Highlights of the district include the Museum of Ancient Sculpture, which holds an extensive collection of Roman, Greek, Egyptian and Asian sculptures, and pieces from the Medieval, Renaissance and the Baroque periods.

Another important museum is the Museum of World Cultures, which is widely regarded as one of the top ethnological museums in Europe. It was founded in 1904, and its collections hold over 65,000 interesting artifacts, from the continents of North & South America, Asia and Africa.

The Römerberg - Frankfurt's Old Town Center

The Römerberg is found in the heart of the Old Town in Frankfurt, in an oddly shaped pseudo-square. At its center is the Justice Fountain. It's the most picturesque public square in Frankfurt, and the busiest pedestrian area in the city.

There are many attractions to see here, including the Römer, which is a striking complex of 11 old buildings built in the 1400s through the 1700s. These include the Old Town Hall and its Imperial Hall, which once held splendid banquets.

Other noteworthy buildings in the square include St. Nicholas Church, the Church of St. Leonhard and the New Town Hall. There are also numerous Kulturschirn, which are open-front shops that were once quite common in Old Town.

The Old Opera House

The Old Opera House is found in the heart of Opera Square in Frankfurt. It was built in Italian High renaissance style in 1880. In WW II, the building was destroyed, but it was reconstructed and opened again in 1981 as a concert venue.

Oper Frankfurt, the newer opera house, and Schauspiel Frankfurt, a drama theater, share one venue, called Opern-und Schauspielhaus Frankfurt. This venue is located a half mile from the Old Opera House, near the river, on Willy-Brandt-Platz.

The Zeil

This is the premier promenade for pedestrians, and it is a very busy shopping street. On The Zeil, you will find specialty shops, department stores and retail chains, with something for everyone. You can approach it at a leisurely pace, if you like, under the sycamore trees.

5. Eat & Drink

If someone asks you to name the food types in German cuisine, you may think first of bratwurst, sauerkraut and beer.

However, German cuisine has changed. They have revived regional cuisines and cook lighter. Germans appreciate well-prepared, healthy foods. If you love good food, German cooking today will impress you.

Fine Dining Restaurants

Main Tower – approximately $216 USD for two

Main Tower is found on the 53rd floor of a skyscraper. It's a popular high-end restaurant and cocktail bar, with a super view. The floor-to-ceiling 25-foot windows allow you to see all of "Mainhattan".

The cuisine here is part regional and part global. Dinner offers a three-course meal including dishes like beef fillet with macadamia nuts and romaneso, and king prawns with fennel and cauliflower salad. The Tower Lounge and restaurant are open 'til midnight.

Erno's Bistro – approximately $140 USD for two

This small and unpretentious restaurant doesn't seem from the outside like it could be considered among the best of Frankfurt's restaurants, but looks can be deceiving. They specialize in fish, which is flown in frequently from France. They also serve an amazing pheasant. The wine list includes 600 unique choices.

Erno's is closed weekends, during the Christmas and Easter times, and sometimes in the summer, when its prime customers – business executives – are not as likely to be in town.

Zenzaken – approximately $244 USD for two

This restaurant is described as a pan-Asian club, and it does have striking Asian décor. The sushi is excellent, and even beef lovers will find many dishes from which to make their choice, like sliced hangar steak and Japanese barbeque sauce. The cocktails are inventive and tasty, including their lemongrass martini.

Surf 'n Turf – approximately $204 USD for two

This is a staple for steak connoisseurs and business people alike. You'll find it near Grüneburgpark. It's a warm, intimate restaurant, with no crowding of tables, and the wait staff is friendly, knowledgeable and helpful. They import their beef from Nebraska. The highlights of their menu include yellowfin tuna tartare and beef carpaccio with truffles.

Mid-range Restaurants

Altes Zollhaus – approximately $90 USD for two

This building was once the Customs House in 1775, and its style is that of a half-timber house. They serve superb international and traditional German dishes. During the right season, you might enjoy their mushroom or game dishes. People also enjoy their fried calf liver and apple rings. In the summer months, you can opt to dine in their lovely garden. Reservations are recommended.

La Boveda – approximately $80 USD for two

This Spanish restaurant is found in a West End residential building basement. The name, translated, means "wine cellar". Among their favorite dishes are those with clams or mussels, and tapas plates. Their wine menu is extensive. If you're visiting on a weekend, they recommend that you call ahead and get a reservation.

Gerbermühle – approximately $84 USD for two

This beautiful 14th century building was originally a restaurant, then it was used for other purposes. Now it is a restaurant again, with indoor and garden dining, a bar that shows its original stone walls and guest rooms. Their specialty is frankfurters, served with Grüne Sosse. Reservations are recommended if you visit over a weekend.

L'Emir – approximately $68 USD for two

The atmosphere of L'Emir is like stepping into One Thousand and One Nights. Belly dancers perform each Saturday night. Their menu is Middle Eastern, and is heavy on vegetarian dishes. Among the favorite dinners are marinated chops grilled on charcoal and house-made lamb sausage. If you have room for dessert, you'll probably enjoy the apricot pudding with raisins or their baklava, which is a honey and nut layered flaky pastry.

Cheap Eats

Zum Gelmalten Haus – approximately $45 USD for two

There just are not many classic Apfelwein (German apple wine) restaurants left, so you'll be glad you found this one. The building and décor remain as they were in the 1800s, with long tables that actually seat 12 people, along with schmaltzy music and ribbed glasses. You might like to try the tender beef tongue with sauerkraut or the special cheeses with vinegar, oil and onion. Sample the apple wine cider, too. It tastes better as you drink more.

El Pacifico – approximately $22-40 USD for two

This festive, little restaurant serves some of the best Mexican food in Frankfurt. They are famous for their fajitas, chicken wings and salad with grilled vegetables. Their fruity margaritas and tequilas are popular, as well. The dining room is not large, so reservations on weekends are a must.

Langosch am Main – approximately $24-45 USD for two

This vegan and vegetarian spot is eclectic and a unique find in Frankfurt. They serve every meal, from breakfast and lunch to dinner and snacks for late-night. They prepare their food with organic ingredients and offer organic beer and wines. Even their lemonade is garnished with fresh rosemary and mint. Their favorite dishes include Frankfurt Tapas, which is a new flavor if this is your first trip to Germany.

Adolph Wagner – approximately $36-50 USD for two

The dark wood wainscoting and sepia murals make this a quaint and memorable restaurant. It's traditional and touristy, both. The kitchen offers similar German dishes to other taverns', but they're tastier. Try the Tafelspitz mit Frankfurter Grüner Sosse (this is stewed beef with a green herb sauce) or their delicious fresh fish on Fridays. They serve lots of cider but not beer. If you want to eat here on a weekend, you'll need a reservation.

6. Culture and Entertainment

Because of its cultural offerings, the city of Frankfurt has much to offer tourists who wish to gaze back in time at the way life was once lived. The museums in the city are diverse and based on many aspects of culture.

Art galleries and stall-front stores allow you to wonder at the beauty from hand-made goods. Exhibition halls and concert venues boast music and art from the past and present, so you can immerse yourself in the culture of this European city.

The Hauptwache

Translated, this means "the Main Guard", and it's also found in the middle of Frankfurt. It has an eclectic mix of modern and historic structures. The Baroque Guard House is among the more notable buildings. Built originally in 1730, it was once used for housing the militia, once as a prison and then as a police station. Now it is a café.

Saint Bartholomew's Cathedral

This Roman Catholic church was built between the 1200s and 1400s, from red sandstone. At 312 feet, it still stands out among the skyscrapers. Emperors' coronations were held from1562 to 1792 in its election chapel. Beneath the church tower is a sculpture by Hands Backoffem, The Crucifixion.

Art City: The Frankfurt Museum of Modern Art

This museum is seen as one of the most important European galleries for contemporary art. The post-modern building opened in 1991, in the city center. Its vast collection includes more than 5,000 pieces that span from 1960 to today. They represent 450 artists, including Roy Lichtenstein, Francis Bacon and Andy Warhol.

Frankfurt Zoo

The zoo houses over 4,500 animals that represent 450 species, and it covers more than 30 acres. This is actually the second oldest zoo in Germany, and was founded in 1858. Its excellent habitats mimic those that the animals live in naturally. Highlights include the Bird Hall and the Nocturnal Animals House. Fun programs and events are held, including themed tours and family festivals and exhibits.

Frankfurt Night-Life

The City of Frankfurt buzzes with places at party at night, whether you just want to grab one drink or party all night. When you want to catch live shows or relax in a speakeasy joint, you can do it in Frankfurt. Here are a few of the most highly recommended Frankfurt night clubs.

The Fox and Hound

This club is on the West End of Frankfurt. It's a sports bar, and has the atmosphere of a beer garden or an English pub. Mondays are steak &

whiskey nights, and Fridays are Juke Box nights. They have longdrinks and cocktails for happy hour. Many locals will gather at this club to watch their favorite sports teams on the screen.

Silbergold

This is as close to a superclub as Frankfurt offers. It has big crowds and loud music. You'll probably have to wait in line to get in, but once you get past their door staff, you can dance or hang out all night. The DJs play various dance classics and there are different guest artists each weekend on the decks.

Batschkapp

Without any question, this is the best place for live music and a variety of bands. It has been running strong for more than 40 years, and still attracts some of the most acclaimed acts in Germany and all of Europe. On nights without live shows, they host regular club nights.

7. Special Events in Frankfurt

Carnivale   February

The procession for Shrovetide Sunday, or Carnivale, is the largest in the region. Each year, almost 500,000 visitors hit the sidewalks. Traditionally, the spectators reward the marchers with sweets and other types of fun or tasty projectiles.

Frankfurt Winter Festival   March

This is one of the most popular winter festivals in Germany. It offers 150 workshops, six dance floors and four separate parties. The music includes Bachata, Salsa and Kizomba. The after-parties last way after normal and free bus shuttles take you right to the location.

Opera Square Festival   June/July

The Old Opera House has an inscription: "Dem Wahren Schönen Guten". It means "To the true, the beautiful and the good". The culinary festival known as Opernplatzfest, held in the

Opera Square, holds good on this promise. It fills the city space with vitality and urbanity, and the music ranges from pop to jazz music.

Spring Dippemess   **April/May**

Frankfurt welcomes spring with this festival at their Ratsweg Fairground. It's the largest festival of its type in the region. There are market stalls and a folk fare with attractions. It guarantees fun for everyone.

Wäldchestag   **June**

Meaning "Forest Day", this festival is unique to Frankfurt. It has been an unofficial holiday for centuries, celebrating the Whitsun holiday high point. People of all generations leave work by lunchtime or earlier, gather their friends and family, and head to the city forest to celebrate Wäldchestag.

Main Festival   **August**

Main Festival begins on a Friday and includes live music at Römerberg. The 6 PM opening ceremony starts the festival off, in front of the city's Justice Fountain. It's a wine fountain for this occasion. The festival includes shooting galleries, games, rides and children's carousels – something for everyone. The highlight is a wonderful display of fireworks, which brings the festival activities to an end on Monday.

Autumn Dippemess   September

Autumn Dippemess in Frankfurt is held at the Ratsweg Fairground. It's just as popular as Spring Dippemess. There is a large sales market with many stalls, along with fairground attractions and a fun fair – another family friendly festival.

Frankfurt Book Fair   October

This is one of the largest book fairs in the world. You can discover new titles and digital published books here. You can meet your literary idols face to face, and there are many discussions, readings and a gourmet gallery.

Christmas Market   **December**

In terms of size and number of visitors, this is among the largest of Christmas markets in Germany. They have creative and elaborate decorations, a huge Christmas tree, and the scenic backdrop of St. Paul's Square and the Römerberg. It's one of the most beautiful of German markets, too.

New Year's Eve – December 31

Frankfurt parties into the New Year with as much gusto as people anywhere. There are bars in the Kaiserstrasse area, and it's just a few-minute's-walk to the river, where you can best see the fireworks. The footbridges are the best places to enjoy the fireworks.

8. Safety in Frankfurt

Frankfurt is largely a very safe city. Even at night, many areas are fine to walk in. You will still want to be careful where you walk, if you're out at night alone. It's always better to stay with someone else or in a group.

Robberies and petty thefts are the most common crimes in Frankfurt. This is especially true in the red-light district near Hauptbahnhof. It is believed that crime in this area is related to drugs. It's best to avoid the Konstablerwache district, too.

If you head to Rodelheim or Bonames, which are remote suburbs, be aware of groups of young people who hang out in gangs and just want to show strength. There aren't any slums to be wary of, so other areas are fine.

Crimes motivated by political unrest are not common in Frankfurt, since 22%+ of its population are immigrants, and they are integrated into the society.

Conclusion

Even if you only have three days to spend in Frankfurt-am-Main, you'll quickly find that it isn't like any other German city. The skyscrapers will remind you of its nickname of "Mainhattan".

In fact, Frankfurt parallels New York City in another way. The population almost doubles in the daytime work hours. More than 1/3 of the residents don't even have a German passport. This diversity in population means that Frankfurt offers you a lot in the way of cultural offerings and different cuisines.

Frankfurt also has a unique German character, even though it's a bustling cosmopolitan city. The historical architecture and art will show this off well. The city has always been a seat of power, and it's a commercial center with much to interest visitors.

Made in the USA
Las Vegas, NV
21 March 2025

19943093R00036